SON OF A PREACHERMAN

SON OF A PREACHERMAN

INS CHOI

ANANSI

Published in Canada in 2026 and the USA in 2026 by House of Anansi Press Inc.
houseofanansi.com

House of Anansi Press is committed to protecting our natural environment. This book is made of material from well-managed FSC®-certified forests, recycled materials, and other controlled sources.

House of Anansi Press is an eBound Digital Certified Accessible publisher. The ebook version of this book meets stringent accessibility standards and is available to readers with print disabilities.

30 29 28 27 26 1 2 3 4 5

Library and Archives Canada Cataloguing in Publication

Title: Son of a preacherman / Ins Choi.
Names: Choi, Ins, 1974- author.
Identifiers: Canadiana (print) 20260176125 | Canadiana (ebook) 20260176257 |
ISBN 9781487014421(softcover) | ISBN 9781487014438 (EPUB)
Subjects: LCGFT: Drama.
Classification: LCC PS8605.H63 S66 2026 | DDC C812/.6—dc23

Book design: Lucia Kim
Cover photograph: Adam Blasberg

House of Anansi Press is grateful for the privilege to work on and create from the Traditional Territory of many Nations, including the Anishinabeg, the Wendat, and the Haudenosaunee, as well as the Treaty Lands of the Mississaugas of the Credit.

Canada Council for the Arts | Conseil des Arts du Canada | Ontario Arts Council | Conseil des arts de l'Ontario | Certified Canadian Publisher

With the participation of the Government of Canada
Avec la participation du gouvernement du Canada | Canada

We acknowledge for their financial support of our publishing program the Canada Council for the Arts, the Ontario Arts Council, and the Government of Canada.

Printed and bound in Canada

FSC MIX Paper FSC® C100212

CONTENTS

Son of a Preacherman was originally produced for the stage by Pacific Theatre, running April 2–13, 2025, at 1440 W. 12th Avenue in Vancouver, BC, Canada.

The following artists were involved:

INS CHOI	Playwright/Actor
KAITLIN WILLIAMS	Dramaturg/Director
HANEUL YI	Musical Director/Actor/Musician
RACHEL ANGCO	Actor/Musician
BEN ELLIOT	Actor/Musician
JONO KIM	Lighting Designer
JESSICA OOSTERGO	Set and Costume Designer
APRIL STARR LAND	Stage Manager
SHONA STRUTHERS	Sound Engineer
CASSIE UNGER	Apprentice Director

Developed with support from Pacific Theatre including a public reading/fundraiser hosted by Timothy Eaton Memorial Church in Toronto, ON, Canada, on February 24, 2025.

Dedicated to my paternal grandparents, Ahn Sung Il and Reverend Choi Sa Chul.

SON OF A PREACHERMAN

In the spring of 2024, Kaitlin Williams was planning the upcoming season for Pacific Theatre when a play abruptly fell through for whatever reason. She told me they had a spot to fill and wondered if I was willing and had something we could work on together. I had a bunch of poems, songs and stories lying about gathering dust, so I said,

INS
Sure. Okay.

KAITLIN
We'll need a title and an image for the poster.

INS
But we don't have a play yet.

KAITLIN
Yeah, but we need to call it something and have
something to look at for marketing purposes.

INS
But what if it's not good?

KAITLIN

Still gotta call it something.

Some of the material had to do with me talking about my dad and my grandfather as preachers, so I said,

INS

How 'bout we call it *Son of a Preacherman* and I'll send some images from a bunch of the poems.

KAITLIN

Works for me.

Thus began the year-long process of shaping this very personal show. Along the way, Haneul Yi came on board as the musical director and helped me realize the songs more fully. Reverend Jason Byassee hosted a public reading/fundraiser for the show at his church in Toronto. Those who were in attendance were the first audience and provided much-needed funds and encouragement. Mark and Jenny Thompson generously offered their home for Haneul and I to stay at during our time in Vancouver. We then had a week to rehearse and to collaborate with performers Ben Elliot and Rachel Angco for what eventually became a two-week sold-out run. Along the way we ate Korean food in the greenroom, took a chilly morning dip at Kitsilano Beach and shared our songs, poems and stories with one another. It was a restorative and exhilarating time of community and art making for me. Later that year, we were nominated for Jessie Awards in the following five categories: Original Script, Direction, Lighting

Design, Performance in a Comedic Role and Production of a Play, and received an award for Significant Artistic Achievement in Sharing an Empowering Historical Narrative. We won for Original Script.

Wow. How did that happen?

What you're about to read is the script of the play. In my opinion, a play is not words on a page but what happens in a theatre among performers and an audience. It's a living art form in real time. So this is a record of that, and as such there are some stage directions to help visualize what happened and what will happen as I keep touring this play. But there are limits to words on a page: they don't always convey humour or pacing; there are no actions or gestures; the images projected in the show aren't included here; there's no lighting, no set, no smells, no music or songs—words on a page can't replicate the feeling of a room full of people laughing and crying together. But these words are the heart of the play and hopefully can be of service and entertainment. The second half of this book is some bits that didn't make the final edit of the show. I don't know if I'll ever have the opportunity to publish more of my work, so I'm including it here.

I recently read a meditation on Psalm 23 written by playwright Murray Watts called *Anthem For Life*. Now at the age of fifty-two, I was reminded that the Lord is still my shepherd—I still shall not want—he still makes me lie down in green pastures—he still leads me beside still waters—he still restores my soul—and though I walk through the valley of the shadow of death, I will still fear no evil for you are still with me—your rod and your staff they still comfort me—you still prepare a table before me in the presence of my enemies, you still anoint my head with oil—my cup still overflows—surely goodness and mercy will still follow me all the days of my life and I will still dwell in the house of the lord forever.

I think that's how this happened.

—Ins.

An empty theatre.
Audience enters.
Houselights fade down.
Stage lights fade up.
The play begins now.

BIRKENSTOCK JESUS *(SONG)*

If Jesus came to visit us today would he recycle everything he had? Would he wear Birkenstocks or flip flops or Crocs? Would he ban every plastic bag? Would all the dolphins swim free from every tuna casserole? Would all the hungry be fed? Would all the homeless be given a home? And who would Jesus raise from the dead?

If Jesus came to visit us today who would be his opposition? Which religious leaders would conspire with whom? Or rather, who'd be threatened by his mission? Would he weep over all the global conflicts and wars? And how we've become more tribal? He'd have billions of followers all over social media but would he have any disciples?

> What kind of music would he listen to? What kind of shows would he PVR? Would he like Lamar, Lecrae and Lauren Daigle and be a fan of *Jesus Christ Superstar?*

If Jesus came to visit us today how would he react to the church? Would he respond, "Well done, my good and faithful servants"? Or would he say, "What the—"? Would the church celebrate the visitation of Christ and bake him a cake tall and wide? Would they welcome him with love and tears of joy or would they ask him to remain outside?

What kind of music would he listen to? What kind of shows would he PVR? Would he like Lamar, Lecrae and Lauren Daigle and be a fan of *Jesus Christ Superstar*? What about Bieber and modern worship songs? *(speaking)* Would he be a fan of the movies *Babette's Feast*, *Jesus of Montreal* and *As It Is in Heaven*—which is this great Swedish film about a small-town choir, it's so good, y'all have to see it—*(back to singing)* How would he be and what would he say if he came to visit us today?

GREETINGS

Good evening. Thank you for being here. My name is Ins Choi. I'm a writer, an actor, I'm the father of two, the husband of one, and true to the title of this show, I am indeed the son of a preacherman. I'm also the grandson of a preacherman, the nephew of a preacherman and the nephew of a preacherwoman.

Three of my female cousins are preachers as well as four of my male cousins. I know—Holy family! What happens when we all get together? Not a lot of listening, that's for sure. *(rimshot)*

I am what is known in the industry as a PK—a preacher's kid/ pastor's kid. Any PKs in the audience? Well, we're in good company cuz you know who else is a PK? Denzel Washington, Nina Simone, Ingmar Bergman, Lewis Carroll, John Boyega from *Star Wars*, Adam Driver also from *Star Wars*, Vincent van Gogh, not from *Star Wars*, Dorothy Sayers, Alice Cooper, Marvin Gaye, Aretha Franklin and the Pointer Sisters.

(a blast of the Pointer Sisters song "I'm So Excited")

Now, PKs are stereotypically either super rebellious or damn near perfect; heaven-sent or hell-bent. We grow up constantly wondering if our parents love the church more than us, feeling guilty if the "family business" isn't well attended and being keenly aware of all the other parents at church always watching us, observing us, judging our every move.

It's this unique situation where the PKs, without intending to, sort of set the standard of what is deemed acceptable in any given church community. The preacher and the preacher's spouse are the examples for the adults, so, it follows, the PKs must be the examples for the kids, right? Nope. We were not exemplary in any way. My eldest sister—I have two older sisters, and the elder one would always go at it with my mom Sunday morning over what to wear to church. It was not the day of rest but the day of war. An early struggle had to do with wearing sneakers instead of dress shoes. Then once that battle was won, it turned to wearing pants instead of a dress, then jeans instead of pants, then slightly ripped jeans, very ripped jeans, skirts, minier skirts, makeup, jewelry, rubber bracelets, combat boots, ripped clothing—essentially Cyndi Lauper, Madonna and the Pointer Sisters.

(a blast of the Pointer Sisters song "I'm So Excited")

And my parents would always force me to be friends with the new kids at church … which isn't a bad thing. In fact, it would've been a great thing if the new kids wanted to be friends with me. It was like setting up kids on these awkward blind dates at church. And honestly, quite a vulnerable position to be in week after week. So much so that I think it kinda messed me up a little with regards to making friends. I'm not that good at it. Don't know if it's a guy thing or a getting-older-as-a-guy thing but my preference is to be alone. I know it's not good to be alone, but I don't think my parents were good at friendship either. I only saw them with other adults when it was work-related, church-related, or if they were related.

Jesus too, come to think of it. Not many friends. Followers, disciples, sure. But friends to just chill with without the pressure of having to be the Messiah? Same with the prophets. It's a solo gig. *(tavern music)* I always imagined all the prophets getting together, like, at a tavern in the wilderness. Isaiah, Jeremiah and Ezekiel would be at one table cuz they made it to the majors; Deborah, Elisha and Nathan would be at another table cuz for some reason they didn't get a book deal; and all the minor prophets would be in the corner fawning over Samuel cuz he somehow swung a sequel. *(tavern music out)*

I always thought friendship was a natural by-product of necessary time spent with others. But now I'm fifty-two years old and at a point in my life where there's not a lot of necessary time spent with others.

My wife has a lot of friends, though. She's a really good friend. I once told her she puts more into her friendships than she gets out of them. She disagreed and then gave me this funny look cuz, I know, why do I talk about friendship as if it's about making a profit? *(sigh)* I wish—*(music)*

BRUCE LEE'S BEST FRIEND *(SONG)*

I wish I was Bruce Lee's best friend in his movie *Enter the Dragon*. We would take on the entire army on that island. When he would take out his nunchucks, I'd take out all my ninja stars. We would destroy all the bad guys, it wouldn't be that hard. I wish I was …

I wish I was Bruce Lee's best friend in his movie *Return of the Dragon*. We would own the streets of Rome and that wouldn't even be braggin'. When he would face off with Chuck Norris, I'd stand by that alley cat. And if something happened, oh, you know, fo sho, I'd have Bruce Lee's back. I wish I was …

> I wish I was Bruce Lee's best friend
> (He wishes he was Bruce Lee's best friend)
> I wish I was Bruce Lee's best friend
> (He wishes he was Bruce Lee's best friend)
> Bruce Lee's best friend.

I wish I was Bruce Lee's best friend in his movie *Fist of Fury*. With all of our *Chinese Connections*, there'd be no reason to worry. We'd even challenge the *Big Boss*. That's right, we'd be his biggest threat. And you know what else, we'd even win the *Game of Death*, without breaking a sweat. I wish I was …

I wish I was Bruce Lee's best friend
(He wishes he was Bruce Lee's best friend)
I wish I was Bruce Lee's best friend
(He wishes he was Bruce Lee's best friend)
Bruce Lee's best friend.

But if I got in a fight right now I'd probably get my head kicked in. I wouldn't know what to do. I'd be so scared cuz I know I'm a chicken. But if I was the best friend of a kung fu fighting champion I wouldn't have to fight. I wouldn't be scared, I'd be alright. And yet people would think I was just holding back my fight.

I wish I was Bruce Lee's best friend
(He wishes he was Bruce Lee's best friend)
I wish I was Bruce Lee's best friend
(He wishes he was Bruce Lee's best friend)
Bruce Lee's best friend.
Bruce Lee's best friend.

ASIAN ROLES AND ROLE MODELS

When I was a kid, the only Asian male I saw on TV was Bruce Lee. Oh, and David Suzuki. Those were my options—a kung fu fighter or an environmental scientist. But I sucked at math and was scared of fights, so what was I supposed to do? Oh wait, there was that other Asian male on TV—he lived on Sesame Street? Bert, from Bert and Ernie? Sure he was Asian, what are you talking about? Black hair—Asian. Yellow skin—Asian. Turtleneck with a striped shirt—come on! Alright, that was a bit of a stretch—never seen an Asian with a monobrow before. But that only goes to show the extent to which my desperation went to connect with someone who looked like me on TV. But some of that's on me cuz all I ever watched was pro wrestling.

(music) The body slam, the pile driver, the suplex, DDT, figure four leg lock, clothesline, off the top rope, one, two, three, ding ding ding. *(music out)* All recess long we'd mimic the posturing, the slogans, the signature moves of these musclebound ultra-masculine men in tight spandex groping each other in creative ways. Everyone wanted to be Hulk Hogan or Ultimate Warrior, but not me. I wanted to be Ricky "The Dragon" Steamboat. He was so cool, so muscular, so good looking, so … Asian. He wore

a red bandana, I wore a red bandana. He wore white tights, I borrowed my sisters' white tights and made it work. My admiration for him grew as he rose in the ranks until he was challenging the Intercontinental Champion, "Macho Man" Randy Savage at Wrestlemania III! Holy smokes, I so wanted to be there. I just had to see it, but it was only available on pay-per-view or if you happened to be in Pontiac, Michigan, that weekend. Must've been real nice living in Pontiac, Michigan, that weekend! The weekend passed with none of us aware of the results. But on Monday morning, it turned out some kid at school actually paid to view and at recess recounted the entire match. Two hundred and fifty wrestling moves, twenty-one false finishes, seventeen minutes of pure adrenaline, pandemonium running wild among the ninety thousand fans eventually cheering for … the new Intercontinental Champion, Ricky "The Dragon" Steamboat! Now all the kids at school wanted to be just like him. I felt so proud, so represented, so Asian.

And then just like that, wrestling was no longer cool. But skateboarding was and among the throngs of blond-haired, blue-eyed, white Southern California skaters was one Christian Hosoi. He was so rad, so wild, so confident—that's right, say it with me … so Asian! I wanted to be just like him. He invented this move called "Christ Air" where he'd launch off a ramp, grab his board, and position himself in the form of a cross mid-air. When I first saw that move, I thought it was a sign from God telling me to be a pro skater. It wasn't. I wasn't that good. But I wanted to be just like him.

Then there was George Takei from *Star Trek*, Pat Morita from *Happy Days* and *Karate Kid*, Michael Chang won the French

Open in tennis, MC Jin was rapping "Learn Chinese." There was Dante Basco from the movie *Hook*, Ke Huy Quan from *The Goonies*, Long ... Duk ... Dong from the movie *Sixteen Candles*. To say the least, Asian male role models in North American media were few, far between and not always flattering.

After I graduated acting school, I was faced with the harsh reality of casting and always being cast in the background because there were no roles for Asian males in the foreground. My illustrious resume includes the likes of Asian Gangster #4 in the background, Chinese Waiter #5 in the background, Vietnamese Band Member in the background playing for white GIs in the foreground—oh, wait, once I played a Japanese security guard in the foreground, that's right ... but I was looking away from the camera to the background ... it was an over-the-shoulder shot, that's right. Not much to write home about. Not much for parents to be proud of. I was very discouraged and losing hope. Then this Asian theatre company invited me to write a play. I never wrote a play before but started writing one about a Korean family and called it *Kim's Convenience*. I figured since Kim was the most popular Korean last name, even if nobody but the Kims in Toronto came out, it would do alright. After years of working on it, I sent it to all the theatre companies in Toronto and they all said no. So I entered it into the Toronto Fringe Festival, which is a do-it-yourself festival, and I did it myself. I'll never forget the end of the very first performance—the lights faded down and it went silent. It must've been a few seconds but it felt like an eternity with only one thought in my head: "They all hate it." When the lights came up, the audience rose to their feet cheering for us. It won the Patrons' Pick award and sold out the entire run. Then the theatre companies who had all said no started calling and the production hit the main stage, selling out shows and touring across the country. Then TV production companies started calling and I was off on a rocket-ship-roller-coaster ride with a steep learning curve full of extreme highs and deep lows. We were celebrated worldwide, winning multiple awards and launching many careers. But the thing I'm most proud of is knowing that a generation of Asian kids, including my daughter and son, grew up watching people who looked like them on stage, on screen, and seeing there's a lot more to being Asian than kung fu, math or being in the background.

WAITING OUTSIDE *(SONG)*

Ask and you shall receive, so the Good Book tells me so
Seek and ye shall find what you're looking for
I've been knocking on this door hoping it'll open wide
But I'm still waiting here outside
Yes I'm still waiting here outside

How long, my God, how long,
Maybe I've been doing this all wrong
Not enough faith, the same mistakes,
Am I just being strung along
Oh Lord look at me. See? I got nowhere to hide
I'm still waiting here outside
Oh yes I'm still waiting here outside

> Please shine your light on me
> It gets so dark I can barely see
> Please draw me close to you
> I feel so alone with no one to turn to
> Has this been all for show
> Just talking to myself with nowhere to go
> No, cuz he said he'd provide

He said I haven't been cast aside
So I'll keep knocking on this door hoping it'll open wide
I'll still be here waiting outside
I'm still waiting here outside

It's okay, one day more, I got it in me
I know, Jesus Lord, you're not finished with me
I'm not gonna get upset, no, I'm not gonna think you lied
But I'm still waiting here outside
Oh yes, I'm still waiting here outside

Please shine your light on me
It gets so dark I can barely see
Please draw me close to you
I feel so alone with no one to turn to
Has this been all for show
Just talking to myself with nowhere to go
No, cuz he said he'd provide
He said I haven't been cast aside
So I'll keep knocking on this door hoping it'll open wide
I'll still be here waiting outside
I'm still waiting here outside

MY GRANDFATHER'S CURSE OF DEATH

(image of Halabujee—grandfather) That's my grandfather. My dad's dad. He was a preacher. He became a preacher much later in life. He was born in 1900, in northern Korea, as it was known back then—this was before the Korean War, before the Japanese occupation. Simply put, the last time Korea was an independent unified country, my grandfather was born and as it turned out, was an only child—which was peculiar at that time cuz in an agrarian society, the more hands you birthed, the less work you had to farm out. So families were huge. But not my grandfather's. He was the only child. So was his dad, and his dad's dad and his dad's dad's dad too. Yeah, three successive generations before my grandfather of only childs and they all died around the age of fifty. Now this unfortunate pattern of only childs dying at around fifty led to suspicions in that town that grew into the firm belief that my grandfather's bloodline was cursed with the curse of death. So with each passing year, he grew more anxious about this curse and its grip on him. Then one day, a Christian missionary came to his town and said,

MISSIONARY

예수님을 믿는다면, 하나님께서 죽음의 저주를 깨뜨려 주실 것입니다.

Y'all get that? Translation please?

MISSIONARY

If you believe in Jesus, God will break the curse of death.

Now those words meant absolutely nothing to most of the audience, but to the good soil of my grandfather's ears, that was not only the Good News, it was Great News—the best news that would not only save his soul but alter the course of his family's cursed bloodline. So my grandfather stood up, went to the front as was instructed, got down on his knees and accepted whoever this Jesus was right there and then.

Then he met her *(image of Halmoni—grandmother)*, a strong, stocky woman of the north who had such large eyes it was rumoured she once literally scared the shit out of a dog just by telling it to "git." Git, shit. Love at first git shit, I guess, cuz they got married, she got pregnant and had a baby boy. "One and done, I guess," perhaps thought my grandfather. But then she got pregnant again and during childbirth that baby died. Then she got pregnant again … and that baby lived. Two boys. And then, three years later, they had a baby girl and then another boy and then another boy—my dad—and then another girl and then another boy and then another girl and then another girl.

Nine mouths to feed, eighteen working hands, twenty-four years between the eldest and the youngest—the family was so big some siblings didn't even know their mom was pregnant before they found out they had a baby sister. As the story goes, my grandmother knew exactly when her final baby would be born. So, she prepared medicinal food that morning, sent the kids to the neighbour's for the afternoon, delivered the baby herself, cut the cord, cleaned herself and the baby, ate the medicinal food while nursing her newborn before calling it a day. Yeah, that kind of fortitude would scare the shit out of me too.

During the Korean War, they brought their family to the south, my grandfather went to seminary, became a preacher and was part of a team that started many churches in the city of Seoul. Some of which are still thriving today.

When my grandfather was nearing fifty, he shared the story about the family curse with my dad, who then shared it with me later on. I think my grandfather was doubtful about how long the curse-breaking power of Jesus would last and wanted to provide an explanation in case he also died at the age of fifty. He lived to be ninety-four years old, with nine kids, twelve grandkids and thirty great-grandkids, some of whom aren't that great. If there ever was a curse, it was broken a long time ago.

Now, I never found out how my grandparents met. My grandmother died before I was born, but I like to think it was at church. *(music)* Maybe at the end of an evening service when everyone was filing out, when things were winding down.

Perhaps she sang in the choir, perhaps he was an usher at the time and maybe it was just the two of them in the sanctuary one magical evening.

AFTER THE LIGHTS TURN ON *(SONG)*

After the lights turn on, the music stops, there's nobody but us
After the money's gone, we're still having fun but what's next for us

You once told me in the end we all walk alone
But the more that I thought about it, I kinda agree, but still I think you're wrong
Cuz I'm with you, you're with me, so we're not alone are we
I'm with you, you're with me, so we're not alone are we

After we become three, our three turns to four and the days keep demanding more
We're always so tired, there's not enough time, we can't remember how we got along before

You once told me in the end we all walk alone
But the more that I thought about it, I kinda agree, but still I think you're wrong
Cuz I'm with you, you're with me, so we're not alone are we
I'm with you, you're with me, so we're not alone are we

(humming break)

After the windows turn blurry, the grinders cease, and it's just us again
After one of us departs or starts to fade away what will become of us then

> You once told me in the end we all walk alone
> But the more that I thought about it, I kinda agree, but still I think you're wrong
> Cuz I'm with you, you're with me, so we're not alone are we
> I'm with you, you're with me, so we're not alone are we

MY DAD

(image of Appa—dad) My dad always wanted to be a preacher. He told me he felt called to be a preacher from an early age. He grew up near the city of Pyongyang in North Korea and on June 25, 1950, when the Korean War broke out—when North Korea attacked South Korea—when North Korea, backed by China and Russia, attacked South Korea; backed by America—which was the situation because at the end of the Second World War—okay so … *(draws a rough map of Asia)* This is Korea, North Korea, South Korea, the capital city of the north is Pyongyang, the capital city of the south is Seoul. This is China, this is Russia, this is Japan. It's not to scale but it'll do. Okay. So, Japan was the first country in the region to modernize, highly influenced by the West—some would even say forced to modernize by the West. So then they got interested in Korea. But China steps in. So Japan wars against China and wins. Then Russia steps in. Japan wars against Russia and wins. And then they annex Korea. Meaning, they just walk right in and take over. So that's 1910. Japan then expands further into Asia until the end of the Second World War, when America drops the atomic bombs on Japan. That's 1945. Then as Japan retreats out of Asia, out of Korea, they inadvertently create a vacuum of power since Korea wasn't

self-governing for the past thirty-five years. So, who would now run things in Korea—the Koreans? Nope. Russia moves in from the north, America moves in from the south, meet at the 38th parallel and decide to rebuild, recreate their respective Koreas in their image—communist in the north, capitalist in the south—and then leave. But they didn't leave. Instead they set the stage for the Korean War. So, on June 25, 1950, North Korea invaded South Korea—

(war music)

APPA

(with Korean accent)

—and in three days they take city of Seoul and in three months they almost take all of Korea except for city of Busan. Then American general Douglas MacArthur do secret plan: take navy behind enemy line, land at city of Incheon and cut off communication line and supply line. Then they start to push communist army back to Seoul, back to 38th parallel, back to Pyongyang, and as they get close to border of China—me and my brother and sister and parents, our family each take one bag and walk from Pyongyang south. But not whole family. My eldest brother, First Born, is in communist army. Third Born, she is in different city working in factory. Fourth Born, he was in high school when communist army come and just take. Yeah, they doing like that. I was Fifth

Born and only fifteen years old, so communist army don't come after me. But they always looking for Second Born but can't find because he dig hole inside home, two feet wide, two feet deep, six feet long—and when communist coming, he hide inside hole, and we put lid on hole, cover with carpet and chair and furniture and we all sit pretend doing something. *(to the actors)* Pretend doing something. And when communist go away, we move chair, rug, lift lid and Second Born come out, stretch, walk around, eat food. Many days he doing like that. *(music)* One day he come home and his eyes is so big, he look like wild animal looking for something. He take string and tie around his finger. Finger turn purple—then he put wood between his teeth, get knife and cut off his finger. Blood streak out. "Ahhhhh!" Then my father come in and see what happen, "Why you do that, why you do that?" He do like that so he don't have to go to communist army. Second Born lead our family to south Korea. Then Chinese army attack and push American army back to 38th parallel. Then next three years, back and forth, back and forth, so many people dying until July 27, 1953, ceasefire. Then Second Born go to seminary become preacher. My father go to seminary become preacher. Me too. I go to seminary become preacher. Then 1975 I come to Canada with my wife, two daughters, In-Ahi,

In-Kyung and my only son, In-Surp, and we
start Toronto Korean Bethel Church.

(images of people at the church throughout the years) It's located in the west end of downtown Toronto in this slowly gentrifying Portuguese neighbourhood. But it wasn't always there. Like many immigrant churches, it began by renting the afternoon slot from a white church until there was some sort of incident; property damage, theological differences, too much kimchee smell in the basement. Then Bethel wandered in the wilderness of Toronto until it reached the promised land downtown. The parents spoke Korean, the kids spoke English and there were always recent immigrant kids who got caught between cultures more than us second-gens.

But wherever we were, every Sunday, I watched my dad get into his costume, take the stage and work his Sunday matinee magic. With his words, his sermon, he was able to make people laugh, cry, feel a sense of purpose, a sense of community. And his sermon always sounded a lot better on Sunday at church than back home during the week as he rehearsed in his tiny office, which was a storage locker he turned into an office with the help of some milk crates, planks of wood and mounds of duct tape. It was equal parts artist studio, the Holy of Holies and that backyard shed from the movie *A Beautiful Mind*. I wasn't allowed in his office ... when he was home, which is how I understood that rule. Cuz when he wasn't home, I'd crack open that stuffy door like Indiana Jones, climb up the tower of milk crates he called a chair, pull on the light, take a sip of his Maxwell House instant coffee elixir before feasting my eyes upon the holy relic—his sermon, the word from God ... which always looked like a complete mess. He handwrote his sermons on paper using different-coloured pens. It was written in Korean with Chinese or English words scribbled once in a while. His penmanship was strong and angled, certain words were circled, others underlined—lines connected this word with that, smearings of liquid paper highlighted the new revisions—it looked like an abstract painting, chicken scratch, a dog's breakfast, but somehow, on Sunday morning, that mess of a page transformed into a holy voice crying in the urban wilderness—a healing balm for the restless soul.

My dad is ninety years old. He's been retired for many years but still has a weekly preaching gig at a long-term care facility with my mom leading worship and continues to work with North Korean refugees. He's been faithful to his calling for his entire life. This is him from a while ago.

(audio recording of Appa preaching)

I REJOICE *(SONG)*

When I'm alone
Not on my phone
I can hear you whispering I'm your song

When I'm surrounded by trees
Aware of the breeze
I can feel you nudging me along

> I rejoice
> Cuz what I thought was chaos was your choice
> To rescue me
> What I believed to be the end was only the start of a new beginning for me

When I lose my voice
Drowning in the noise
I can't remember what you said to me

When I get lost in the crowd
When everything's loud
I close my eyes and catch a glimpse of your shining face on me

I rejoice
Cuz what I thought was chaos was your choice
To rescue me
What I believed to be the end was only the start of a new beginning for me

When all of the dreams you planted in me long ago never seem to grow
Or form in a way that would never suggest they would ever take place
When none of the things I'm making are actually taking
Despair is all I see
You remind me you're still making me

When I look back
On the onslaught of setbacks
I can read between the lines now and see your hand

When I start to dream
Harder now than it seems
I can feel you breathe again and then I understand

I rejoice
Cuz what I thought was chaos was your choice
To rescue me
What I believed to be the end was only the start of a new beginning for me

SON OF A PREACHERMAN

(image of Umma and Appa) That's my parents on their wedding day. Everyone used to say I looked just like my mom but as I got older I started to look more like my dad.

My dad never told me he wanted me to be a preacher. When I was a kid I never felt pressured to be a preacher from my dad … but from my mom? Oh, a thousand percent. She so wanted me to be a preacher. You know how I could tell? She told me all the time.

UMMA

You was born to be preacher. You destiny is to be preacher. The purpose of you life is to be preacher.

Which is a lot of pressure on a five-year-old. But I don't blame her—she kinda had to … cuz she made this deal with God.

See, my mom has high blood pressure. And when she gave birth to my two older sisters she lost so much blood it got dangerous. So my dad was on his way to get a vasectomy when my grandfather stopped him dead in his tracks—confronted him face to face like in the wild west. Now, this was back in Korea so it was the wild east and they spoke Korean, but it might've sounded something like this ...

(music)

GRANDFATHER

Where do you think you're going, preacher-man?

APPA

Where does it look like I'm going, preacher-man? To get a vasectomy. Obviously.

GRANDFATHER

Is that right, preacherman?

APPA

Uh huh, that is right, preacherman.

GRANDFATHER

Well, you've got two daughters by my count, which is fine, but you ain't getting no vasectomy until you have a son. Is that understood, preacherman?!

My dad took a breath, steadied himself and sternly replied,

APPA

Yes sir!

(music out) So he returned to my mom with these new marching orders, but nothing was happening. Shooting blanks. So they prayed to God for help. Nothing. They fasted and prayed. Still nothing. Then my mom prayed Hannah's prayer. Hannah's this woman in the bible who couldn't have kids. So she prayed to God,

(music)

HANNAH

God, if you give me a son, I'll dedicate him to your service.

God hears, Hannah conceives, gives birth to a boy and names him Samuel. Samuel grows up to be one of the most notable prophets in the Bible. So my mom followed suit.

UMMA

God, if you give to me son, then, then, he will be preacherman.

God hears, my mom conceives, has an easy pregnancy, a problem-free labour and gives birth to me. *(music cuts out)* What!? I'm no Samuel! I'm not a prophet! In fact, I'm not for profit! *(rimshot)* But to my mom, I was the answered prayer, the goods delivered, and as I grew, I was the constant reminder of the deal she made with God, which was all about me, which I had no say in! So, she constantly reminded me that one day I was to be a preacher. Now, I don't know about you but if someone tries to make me do something, I usually don't wanna do it. And the more they push, the more I push back. So I fought against being a preacher. But after I graduated high school, I didn't get into university. See, the thing was, I never got good marks in school. My sisters both got good marks, my cousins all got good marks—it seemed like every Asian in Toronto got good marks except for me. I failed as an Asian, didn't know kung fu, had no friends, didn't get good marks. I mean, I always knew I was smart, I just had no proof. So when I received the rejection letters, everyone in my family was discouraged except for my mom.

UMMA

See, I told you. You was born to be preacher. You destiny is to be preacher. The purpose of you life is to be preacher. So hurry up and go to Bible College.

So I did. I was finally ready to fulfill my destiny. But as I leafed through the course catalogue, I saw this class called Acting 101, took it, fell in love with acting and then was torn over what to do with my life. On the one hand, I could become a preacher; I know what that looks like—it's a well-worn path in my family. But on the other hand, this acting thing was more joyful, I felt all my cylinders firing, plus, there was all this necessary time spent with others resulting in the natural by-product known as friends. So I prayed to God for help. Nothing. I fasted and prayed. Still nothing. Then because I was fasting and praying so much, I got tired and fell asleep and dreamed that Jesus came to me and flicked me on my forehead.

INS

(flick)

Ow. Jesus.

JESUS
Yeah?

INS
Oh, hey, yeah, hi, so, I don't know what I'm supposed to do with my life. People keep telling me you have some kind of plan for me, but you don't seem to be communicating it very clearly. *(flick)* Ow.

JESUS
Listen, I'm with you all the time. I just want you to be with me. That's it.

INS
But what do I do?

JESUS
Well, what do you like doing? What are you good at?

INS
I like acting and writing creatively. I think I'm pretty good at that.

JESUS
Then go and do that. *(flick)*

So I dropped out of Bible college, sanctioned by Jesus, and miraculously got into acting school. I also moved out of my parents' house cuz I felt like God was calling me to depend more on him than my parents. Like, if God is calling me to be an actor, an artist, then that's what I'm doing and come what may, God will provide, right? Well … money was always tight and it wasn't easy, but I tumbled through and graduated, moved downtown, got an agent and started auditioning.

And with every unbooked gig, my confidence waned, and with each passing year, I grew more frustrated and doubtful about this path I was on. And then one summer, in my late twenties, I went to a friend's wedding. This guy I grew up with.

CHANG
Ins!

INS
Hey. Congratulations on your wedding. You did it. You finally tricked someone into marrying you.

CHANG
Nice of you to dress up for my wedding, bro.

INS
Sorry, just came from rehearsal.

CHANG
A movie?

INS

No but it's this really interesting play—

CHANG

You bring anyone? Want me to make some introductions? The harvest is plentiful, bro—

INS

No, I'm good.

CHANG

No, you're not.

INS

You got people to see. I'll let you go.

CHANG

Wait. Ins, I respect you bro, but it's my wedding and someone's gotta say it.

INS

What?

CHANG

What the hell you doing with your life? It's time to cut bait and adult up. You may look at me and all you see is a cop. But it's a steady income, benefits—What are you doing?

INS

I'm writing a play about a Korean family and their convenience store?

CHANG

Dude, it's time to wake up. Do you know what I do?—Oh my God, bro, you'd be perfect. I'm in recruiting, I recruit people to be cops. It's like acting. I give presentations. Why don't you do what I do? I'll hire you. You never have to shoot anybody, I swear, and there's a steady paycheque, benefits, a pension—

INS

I appreciate it, but no thanks.

CHANG

Just think about it. I'm gonna follow up.

He never followed up, but I did think about it a lot. Then one day my dad asked me for help. A bunch of kids from his church were going ice skating and they needed some adult supervision. So all day long I tied skates, taught kids how to stop, turn, and then the strangest thing happened—God called me to serve those kids. That's as clear as I can put it. My dad's church was looking for a part-time children's pastor and since I was a full-time out-of-work actor, I auditioned and got the part. I fell in love with those kids and served them for six years with all my creativity and imagination. Then the church wanted me to attend seminary. I didn't want to but obeyed and slowly graduated.

Then my dad retired and the new preacher wanted me to come on board full-time. I didn't want to but obeyed, and at the end of that harrowing year, I was burnt out, lacked support, and that new preacher ended up leaving cuz he didn't get along with the elders and another preacher came on board. But by then I was asking myself, "How did I get here?"

I didn't want to be a preacher. I fought against being a preacher. I chose not to be a preacher and yet here I was, smack dab in the middle of Destiny's hand, a preacher. One evening I was at church, I was in the upper room in front of this big stained glass window. It was raining outside when my dad walked in.

APPA
Oh. What you doing here so late?

INS
Hey Appa, just sorting through all these lost and found items. Kids don't know how valuable things are.

APPA
Yeah, you used to lose lots of thing too. House key, wallet, one time you even lose report card. You remember? Mm-hm.

INS
Hey, Appa, can we talk?

APPA

What we doing now, not talking?

INS

Well, I've been working here for a while and ... I don't know, I was thinking maybe it was time to move on.

APPA

Move on? Work at different church?

INS

Not so much a different church as a different chapter in my life. I'm not a preacher, Appa.

APPA

What's wrong?

INS

God didn't make me to be a preacher. He made me to be creative, to use my imagination, to make things.

APPA

Make sermon. Make disciple. Church work is hard work. Nothing is easy. Halabujee (*Grandfather*) do that, I do that.

INS

I'm not Halabujee, Appa. I'm not Kunabujee

(*Second Born*), Inho, Injoon, Jinsook, Sam, Gomo, I'm not you. You always felt called to be a preacher. And that's great. You've been so committed to that your whole life. But I feel like God is calling me to act and write.

APPA

Yeah, that's preacher—

INS

No, like on a stage in front of an audience—

APPA

Yeah, that's preacher.

INS

No, like—

APPA

You start, you finish. What you talking. Church work is hard work. Nothing is easy. No. No!

(Music begins and swells, then simmers to a single note)

DRAGONFLY *(SONG)*

Timid and shy
Just trying to get by
Keep your head down, keep swimming around
No need to ask why

It's safer on the edges
Minding your own business
Keep it low and slow, in the shadows
And no one will notice

Then one day you cling to
Or rather something clings to you
And you climb up to where
There's no water, just air
And suddenly you feel dry
The air makes it so dry
You begin to crack cuz you're so dry
You want to break out and cry and try to pry oh my it feels like you die

Then you fly
Huh?
You're flying
What? How?
How is this happening
I don't know
Wow—You're in the sky now
I don't get it

When did you get wings
I know, I don't know
Are you imagining
This is so weird,
You're so strange, you're so odd, so intense, oh my God—
Now your name finally makes sense

You're so much more
Than what you thought was in store
All you went through
You were always meant to
You thought you died
But you were being
Clarified, purified, refined as a dragonfly

FINAL THOUGHTS

(music continues) I don't know how to think about the deal my mom made with God. I mean, technically, I think I made good on it as there was no length of time stipulated in the contract, so ... And who knows the future. Maybe there's a creative pulpit somewhere with my name on it, but I didn't become a preacher. I remained an artist and have been working with my imagination for my whole life.

My daughter is seventeen years old and my son is fifteen. To the frustration of my wife, they're a lot like me. Not sure if either of them will become preachers, but if they do, my mom will be very happy. Maybe it skips a generation. And if they don't want to go into acting or writing, that's okay, just as long as they become a doctor or a lawyer or an engineer. Kidding. Engineers don't make as much money as they used to. I hope they discover what they enjoy doing, what they're good at, what God has invested in them, and double down on that.

These are my parents. *(image of Umma and Appa today)* When *Kim's Convenience* premiered at the Fringe Festival in 2011, six years after I stopped preaching, my parents came to see it. Afterward they came up to me and hugged me and my dad said,

APPA

Thank you. We are so proud of you.

Life is short. And whether you believe in destiny, fate, or God's will, life is also what you make of it. So …

GET STARTED *(POEM)*

Get started
Get started before you get hard-hearted
Get started before your dearly beloved becomes dearly departed
Start it
I know it's hard
Starting is hard
It's hard to start
It might be the hardest part
Starting
From nothing to something
Something from nothing
Cuz you can do something with something
Something can be done if there's something there
But nothing's nothing
It's a different thing
It's a lack of a thing
It's no thing
What do you do with no thing?
What can you do?
Nothing
There's nothing you can do with nothing

But order another coffee
Check another email
Scratch another sensible itch
And as offence turns to defence
Creation turns to maintenance
And bam
Nothing's back
But once you start
Just like that
Nothing's gone
That taunting void is silenced
The spell is broken and the despairing abyss of a blank page
urging you to relent, vanishes
And don't worry, craft will come later
Yes, rigor will come later
I promise you, rhythm, reason, rhyme will all come later
But for now, no matter how bad that plot is
Or if the horse is in front of where the cart is
Know your supple heart is where your start is and get started

Good
Not too much
Just enough
Less
Way less
What are you doing?
Don't rob the audience of their role
Cuz it's not for you
It's for them
Don't forget that

You're doing this for them cuz you love them
And you're almost there
I know you've been almost there for a long time but stop now and it's a poorly told story
That's not a threat nor a denial of how hard this is
That's what usually happens cuz poorly told stories are brazen survivors fearing no one, fighting tooth and nail to exist on your page, arrogantly confident that you'll tire and give up
Whereas a story well told is that rare invitation awakening us to where we were going and why
The world needs your story
And your story needs you to tell it well

Good
I think it's time to let go
Time to magnify something else
It's been a comforting return
Here
These pages
A familiar place to go to no matter how you feel, where what you do is immensely appreciated by your future self, I'm with ya
But now it's time for you to let go
Of course they may hate it or not care
And yes, you will be found out
You will be known
But it's not for you, remember? It's for them
So
Go ahead *(extend an arm with a tight fist)*
Nice and easy
There you go

Keep going *(slowly open the fist)*
You're almost there
That's it *(stretch fingers out, exhale)*
Good
Well done

Stage lights fade down.
Curtain call with music.
Performers exit the stage.
Houselights fade up.
Audience exits the theatre.
An empty theatre.
The play ends here.

SOME BITS THAT DIDN'T MAKE THE FINAL EDIT

These are stories, song lyrics and poems that flirted in the mix as I was making this play but were cut for various reasons. I still love them. So I included them here. Some of these pieces, along with many that are in the play, were birthed from gatherings called Makers Collective. From time to time I've gathered groups of artists (writers, songwriters, visual artists, etc.) to make new works in response to passages in the Bible. It's usually a gathering of about eight folks, either in person or online, committed to meeting five times within the span of a couple of months. I choose a scripture passage and people share a new piece each time we gather. It builds community for a time, provides a deadline and forces us to wrestle with scripture.

Hope you enjoy them.

ELDERS *(SONG)*

This was written in a Makers Collective in response to the Book of Ruth—the part where a group of elders discuss aspects of their laws that may threaten the union of the two main characters who are in love.

We are elders of this community
We've been gathered for the sake of our unity
Sometimes motives hide
And lawsuits divide
And by then we've lost our opportunity

We have witnessed many transactions
Some funny customs involved in these actions
We don't mean funny ha ha
But funny like "what the—?"
We'll try to provide explanations

We are gathered at the gate
We are ten in number
We are the elders with ears to hear
We are pondering their fate

We are men in wonder
We are the witnesses here

Now, this matter before us is tricky
It involves a few laws that are sticky
Leviticus 25
Helps the poor survive
But depends on their family's generosity

Deuteronomy 25:6
Raises a problem which it tries to fix
Your brother dies without children
It's your duty to make them
With his wife. And hope things all click

We are gathered at the gate
We are ten in number
We are the elders with ears to hear
We are pondering their fate
We are men in wonder
We are the witnesses here

Now we don't know why sandals are removed
Nothing's gained. Nothing's improved.
But we do it anyway
Cuz at the end of the day
It seals the deal, approved

May our heavenly Lord make this woman
Although she's, from the looks of it, foreign

Like Leah and Rachel
Who built up Israel
May she be so blessed with children
Like Leah and Rachel
Who built up Israel
May she be so blessed with children

PRAYING TO SEE

This was written in a Makers Collective in response to the Sermon on the Mount—the part about praying.

I used to think if I opened my eyes while I was praying, the Spirit of God would melt my face like in that scene from the movie *Raiders of the Lost Ark*. Indiana Jones and Marion are tied to a pole, back to back, and he advises her to close her eyes—she does—the Nazis then open the Ark of the Covenant and ghouls fly out, melting the faces of those whose eyes are open. As if closed eyes functioned as bloodstained doorposts at the first Passover, or like a scarlet thread on the walls of Jericho, or like that time God put Moses in a crack and covered him until He passed by—Moses got a gander of God's backside, which didn't melt his face but left him with a holy glow.

So whenever I prayed as a kid, I'd clench my eyes like a fist and place my hands over them just to make sure they wouldn't open even by accident. But sometimes the prayers went long at my dad's church—the Korean church where he was the head pastor—where the elders believed the length of the prayer was directly proportional to their holiness; the longer they prayed, the holier they got and the drowsier the congregation became. It's hard to keep your eyes closed for that long when you're eight years old and don't understand Korean very well—or at any age cuz those prayers were long—and sometimes they'd go for ten, twenty, thirty minutes—I'm not kidding. We were hostages being tortured by these odd monologue performance art pieces every Sunday matinee.

So, to combat the temptation of sneaking a peek during these marathon prayers, I started doing eyeball exercises. Behind my hands, under my clenched eyelids, I'd move my eyeballs left and right … up and down … do circles, clockwise, then counter-clockwise … spirals from the circumference toward the centre and back out … horizontal figure eights, vertical figure eights—any pattern I could think of, really. And once in a while, when I'd position my pupils to the left then pan quickly to the right, I'd see something.

That's right

With my eyes closed

I'd see a flash of something.

Try it right now. You'll see it. Close your eyes and look to the far left then look quickly to the right.

See? A flash in the middle. Like a pulse or like an orb of light—like a fuzzy photo taken by the Hubble space telescope of some distant galaxy. And I'd start to think maybe this is some kind of message, like in the movie *Contact*, some extra-terrestrial being trying to communicate to me through this pulsing light whenever I closed my eyes in church to pray.

ELDER
Amen.

The marathon prayer would conclude with echoes of "Amen" filling the sanctuary, repeated by those who were still awake. Meanwhile, those of us dead in Christ would slowly lift our heads from off the pew in front of us and safely open our sticky eyes. The service continued but the lid was back on the Ark, the walls of Jericho had fallen, God had passed by and I'd be left with my eyes wide open, basking in the light of a holy glow.

A HOLE *(SONG)*

The more I take from it the bigger it gets
The more I put in it the smaller it gets

It's only there when something's removed
When it appears it cannot be moved

If it's in a boat, that boat won't float
If it's in my head, I'm probably dead

What I'm singing about
Is a hole, a hole, like a hole in the ground
A hole, a hole, they're usually round
A hole, a hole, holy moly! It's totally a hole
It's how I'm making this sound ooooo

You cannot hold it but you can go through it
You may be in it but you cannot see it

It's in a doughnut but not in a dutchie
It's in Eight, Six, Nine and Zeeeeeero.

What I'm singing about
Is a hole, a hole, like a hole in the ground
A hole, a hole, they're usually round
A hole, a hole, holy moly! It's totally a hole
It's how I'm making this sound ooooo

In outer space it's wormy or it's black
It's sometimes called a cavity, an opening or a crack
I'm left with it when pricked by a thorn
Through it all babies are born

Bubbles are formed because of it
Instruments need it, that's definite
Sometimes it's squishy and sometimes it's hard
It's necessary in golf and billiards

What I'm singing about
Is a hole, a hole, like a hole in the ground
A hole, a hole, they're usually round
A hole, a hole, holy moly! It's totally a hole
It's how I'm making this sound ooooo

A HIGHFALUTIN' BIBLE COMMENTARY

This was written in a Makers Collective in response to Ecclesiastes 3:5, "A time to cast away stones, and a time to gather stones."

Yeah, I have no idea what this verse is talking about. Cast away stones? Gather stones? First of all, how big are these stones? Cuz that sounds like a lot of work. Secondly, how big are stones compared to rocks? I mean, geologically speaking, on Saturday mornings, Pebbles was Fred Flintstone's daughter, so flint stones are bigger than pebbles, but Barney Rubble worked at Slate Rock and Gravel Company, so I'm leaning toward rocks then gravel then stones then rubble then pebbles. Bam bam. Got it.

I assume it has to do with some sort of ancient Jewish agricultural practice—casting stones, gathering stones. Most mysterious references in the Bible do. Either that or it's about sex. I mean, the last time I gathered stones and cast them away was at the beach, skipping them with my kids. And yes, it takes "a time" to find the right kind of stone—thin but not too thin, circular and heavy enough to fling but not too heavy. And if you don't take "a time" to gather the right kind of stone, they don't "cast" right, they don't skip. You're then just frustratingly throwing stones in the water with your kids looking up at you wondering what "skipping" should look like.

Why would you cast away stones in the first place?

My second-oldest sister is a bit of a hoarder. She still has a stone collection from when we went to Florida forty years ago. I'm sure it's crossed her husband's mind to cast those stones away. And I imagine you would have to cast stones away from your field before you started planting seeds if you were a farmer. Someone on the internet said you would cast stones into your enemy's field so their crops wouldn't grow. But then now you're gathering stones from your field cuz someone did that to you? Well, serves you right. Another person on the internet wondered if these were precious stones, meaning there's a time of debt where you have to sell your gemstones—cast them away—and a flush time in your life when you're gathering them. Casting stones was also a form of judgement. So there's that.

Well, this verse is part of a list that illustrates the seasons of human activities. The list is set up by the phrase "To everything there is a season, a time for every purpose under heaven." Also the Hebrew word "hevel," usually translated as "meaningless" or "vanity," occurs thirty-six times in this book. Meaning it's a big theme of the book. But that word literally means "vapour" and one Rabbi on the internet translates it as "impermanence." So one sobering interpretation of this verse could be that complete control of our lives and ultimate fulfillment in this life are an illusion. Learn to enjoy the moments as your life ebbs and flows. So … there's a time to cast away stones, whatever that is, and try to enjoy it but don't get too used to casting stones cuz it's impermanent and now it's time to gather stones. Hey! It's not my fault and you're not in control either. So stop griping about how good it was when we were casting stones a moment ago and start gathering stones. Look, if you hate gathering stones so much, don't despair, cuz this too is impermanent and before you know it, we'll be casting stones again with the best of 'em. But don't expect casting stones to give your life ultimate meaning, cuz you'll only be disappointed.

Yeah, still not completely satisfied with that, but that's what I've gathered and them's the stones I'm casting.

VANITY OF VANITIES *(POEM)*

This was written in a Makers Collective in response to the Book of Ecclesiastes.

Vanity of vanities
All of this humanity
Staring at insanity
Grasping for the wind

Vanity of vanities
Like a drowning manatee
Cursing lewd profanities
Much to my chagrin

It's like a bare-assed bear who was embarrassed for his lack of hair who then went off to who-knows-where and found a hare that matched his hair who sounded hounded, quite astounded, pounding grounds that were unfounded when the bear proposed to wear the hare as his new derriere.

Vanity of vanities
All of this humanity

Staring at insanity
Grasping for the wind

Vanity of vanities
Like a drowning manatee
Cursing lewd profanities
Much to my chagrin

It's like a can of peas under a canopy of trees that cannot see the Pleiades and so believe it cannot be. But when all the leaves that make the canopy of trees begin to fall it opens up to all and not just like a conference call with protocols and wherewithals at City Hall or shopping malls that clog up like cholesterol but opens up like waterfalls of space to see the overall in place which can appease the can of peas to then perceive the Pleiades.

Vanity of vanities
All of this humanity
Staring at insanity
Grasping for the wind

Vanity of vanities
Like a drowning manatee
Cursing lewd profanities
Much to my chagrin

PLEASE GOD

This was written in response to Psalm 116:4, "Lord, save me."

I transferred to a new high school when I was in grade eleven cuz it was closer to home. It was also because I wasn't doing so well at my previous school. After I transferred, I auditioned for the school musical and got a part. It was still the first semester, and I thought it'd be a good way to make friends but rehearsals wouldn't begin until the second semester, so I usually went home for lunch—didn't want to sit alone in the cafeteria. At home I'd make Shin Ramyun cuz it was quick and easy. Throw in a couple of hotdog wieners, crack an egg in and just before it fully cooked, slide in a slice of cheese to creamify the broth. I ate it out of the pot with some kimchee while watching reruns on TV. After I was done, I'd wash the pot and the two chopsticks, turn off the TV, lock the door and return to school.

Chemistry class followed lunch and over the course of that first semester, I slowly fell behind with no way of catching up. I should've asked for help. But I wasn't comfortable talking to teachers. I always felt they were trying to make me look stupid. Plus, I was very shy and proud and didn't want to let on how much I didn't know—oh, right—that's also why—cuz my previous school was a term school, so that meant eight subjects a day for the whole school year. But this new school was semestered—four subjects for the first half of the year—which meant more content was being covered per class. So, even if you missed one class, or forgot to do your homework one time, or were feeling sluggish and not paying attention in class cuz of the super-hearty Shin Ramyun you just had for lunch, it quickly snowballed into an avalanche of silent desperation and freezing anxieties until … there I was in the middle of the hallway at the end of the semester about to write my final chemistry exam like a snowball in hell.

Okay, so, y'know what? I don't even know why I was taking chemistry in the first place. Like, who made that choice? I don't ever remember saying, "I wanna take chemistry." Like, why was I enrolled in that class? I wasn't gonna be a chemist. That was my first question. Second, why were we even studying chemistry? Like, at all. Why was that even taught in school? I've never used chemistry in my life since I graduated high school. Never. Nor, while I'm at it, all the math I had to learn. Algebra? Nope. Quadratic equations? Nope. Never. Advanced functions, calculus, vectors, polynomials, trigonometry, n-e-v-e-r e-v-e-r! The only math I've ever had to do was to divide the price of a box of four ice cream sandwiches by four to get a per-unit price to compare that against a box of six ice cream sandwiches. There's four people in my family. And by the way, the box of six ice cream sandwiches ends up being a lot cheaper. But then those two extra ice cream sandwiches end up sitting at home in the freezer, becoming more of a nuisance than a dessert. So, I'll decide to take one for the team and eat one but then there's only one left, so fine, I'll eat that too. Which then makes me feel horrible cuz I just ate two ice cream sandwiches just to get rid of them. Then all of a sudden, my kids show up out of nowhere and ask accusingly, *Hey! Who ate the ice cream sandwiches?* To which I reply, *You snooze, you lose!* Cuz if it rhymes then it sounds more like a real thing of parental wisdom.

Where was I? Right, about to write my final grade eleven chemistry exam and I wasn't ready. I was so scared. So, I prayed,

INS
God, I know, I know, I know, yup, totally, I get it, uh huh, for sure, absolutely, hundred percent, yeah, yes, yes and yes … but, y'know? If you could just, I mean, like, I just, I could really, uh, please, God? Please help me?

The exam began and I read the first question. I didn't understand it. So I read it again and still didn't understand it. I started panicking cuz I didn't even know what the question was asking. The other students were writing no problem. So I skipped that first question and went to the second one, but it looked like it was written in Chinese. I didn't understand what I was looking at. A cold sweat of panic shivered through my body as I skipped that question and looked at the third.

INS
Thank you, God.

I understood it and even knew the answer. I wrote that down as quickly as I could before it fell out of my head. Then the fourth question I also knew. I started feeling a bit better.

INS

Two questions down. That's not bad considering—huh? A student left her seat? Guess she had to ask the teacher about something, but you're not supposed to get up at all. She's gonna be in trouble. What? She handed in her exam? How can she be done already? I'm just—it's only been—and she's finished? Well, she's not impressing anybody, I'll tell you that much, cuz it's not a race, missy, Miss Brown-Nosing, Little Miss Trying-to-Impress-the-Teacher-by-Finishing-Her-Exam-So-Fast.

Then more students finished and left. And then more students finished and left. And as I ventured through all the questions, trippingly finding a path through this dense exam, I finally came up for some air and discovered I was the last student left. Wow. Time had never moved so furiously.

My answers weren't getting any better, so I gave it a final review and handed it in. I left the classroom, walked down the hall, got my jacket from my locker and went outside. I was spiralling in a whirlwind of desperate failing thoughts when I heard a voice.

THIS GUY

Ins, was it?

I turned and saw this guy I met at the school musical callbacks.

INS
Hey.

THIS GUY
Which exam you just write?

INS
Chemistry.

THIS GUY
How'd you do?

INS
I dunno. You never know with these things.

THIS GUY
Yeah. *(beat)* We're gonna go get something to eat. Wanna join us?

INS
Uh, yeah, sure. I could eat.

So, I joined him and his friends and we walked to the food court at the local mall. We got a bite to eat then wandered in and out of stores pretending to be interested in the merchandise, talking about movies, music, sport teams. It was a nice time. We wished each other well and went our separate ways.

I failed the chemistry exam.

God didn't answer my prayer.

I prayed to God for help and it didn't work. God didn't miraculously come through for me. There was no parting of the Red Sea, no manna in the wilderness, no water turning into wine; the deaf didn't hear, the blind didn't see, the lame just continued to be lame—I didn't study and I failed the exam. That's it. That's what happened. God didn't hear me or God didn't care or prayer didn't work. That was the takeaway. *(sigh)* I mean, what's one chemistry exam in the grand scheme of things, right? Sure, but still—even the sparrow, right?

Anyway, the second semester began and I no longer came home for lunch. Each morning I packed a meal, took it to school, stored it in my locker and when it was lunchtime, I went to the cafeteria, sat down and ate it with my new group of friends—the cast of the school musical that I was getting to know during rehearsals. I never prayed for friends, but with groanings too deep for words, it was for which my soul was so desperately aching.

REMEMBER HIM? *(POEM)*

This was written in response to the eleventh station in the Stations of the Cross. I imagine this poem to exist in the mind of an observer after the second criminal on the cross says to Jesus, "Lord, remember me when you come into your kingdom."

Remember him?
Why?
What for?
What he do?
He somebody?
He invent something?
He do a lot of good with his life?
He's up there for some reason
Sure, could be unjust punishment but just because you're unjustly punished don't make you worthy of remembrance
If that were the case, hey, get in line, there's trillions of us and who's to say what's unjust?
It's a desperate plea in the midst of a public execution, that's all, understandable, for sure, I'd probably do the same, but that's all it is
Survival instincts kicking in

A little insurance request at the end taking full advantage of who he happened to be hung beside
Move on
Not worth it, Jesus
Besides, that wouldn't be fair
How would that be fair?
How would that be just?
What about everybody else?
You gonna remember them too?
He's getting what he deserves
Done
Kaput
Kuman
Finito
Case closed
What, he's gonna do something for ya?
You think he's got great potential hanging there like a bloody billboard sign?
Gonna advertise you?
Be of benefit to you somehow enough to make it worth it?
No
None of that is happening
Definitely not
He's just gonna hang there naked until he runs out of air
That's it
A cautionary tale for what happens to bad people
That's what's happening
He's got a hundred breaths left, if that, with no opportunity to do any good for you even if he could
Even if he wanted to, he's no use to you

You don't gain by remembering him
In fact, you lose
He'll make you look bad
Look at him
He looks bad
He looks shameful
He'll only defile, tarnish, shame your name
Bring you down
Smear it all in and stink it all up
He's only thinking of himself, after all, with that audacious, impudent, brazen request to be remembered
What about that other guy?
That's not rewardable behaviour, thinking only for himself
Forget him
He's nobody
Stop wasting your time
Jesus, don't remember him

YOU REMEMBER ME *(SONG)*

This was written in a Makers Collective in response to the story of Jonah.

Hey, yeah, it's me again
I keep finding my place and then
I keep forgettin' why, where I was headin'

Oh right, sorry, yes, yes, I know,
I was meaning to call but then I lost control of my circumstances
then I missed my chances to call

I'm losing track
Of why I'm back
To where I was before
I get so distracted
Always attracted
To that something more
I keep forgetting who I am
Made to be
And although I forget
You remember me

Alright, I get it, well, here's the thing
I was managing my time well when things got happening
Then it really picked up
And I couldn't keep up with all the jugglin'

Okay, hey, what do you want me to say
I'm just cluttered in my thoughts, I'm not running away
From you
No, no, no that's just not true
I just have so much to do

I'm losing track
Of why I'm back
To where I was before
I get so distracted
Always attracted
To that something more
I keep forgetting who I am
Made to be
And although I forget
You remember me

MINE EYES ARE LEAN *(POEM)*

Mine eyes are lean
See?
Lean
That's all
But that don't mean how I see is lean or small
Don't mean what I foresee can't be big and tall
Don't mean what I envision has to be infinitesimal
Don't mean nothin'
Ain't no thing
They just lean, that's all
But y'know
The funny thing is
Because mine eyes are lean
Sometimes
I can't be seen
Sometimes
I don't get seen
When I audition
I get pre-screened
Deemed unclean
Too obscene for the big stages, the glossy pages, the silver screen

When I audition
I get Asian Gangster #4 in the background
Chinese Waiter #5 in the background
Vietnamese Band Member in the background playing for white
GIs in the foreground
Oh, once I got Japanese Security Officer in the foreground
That's right
But I was looking away from the camera to the background
It was an over-the-shoulder shot
That's right

If only mine eyes were larger
Maybe then it wouldn't be so hard or
Maybe then I could take charge or
Barge in from outside the margin like Sgt. Slaughter
Charging to go farther ahead
Further
Instead of just beginning to begin
Every inning
No win
Never winning
No in
Just copin'
Constantly mopin' bout the system being all broken
Scopin' for any open door
Hoping there's got to be more than Chance's grope
Panting for hope
Dancing to all those multicultural diversity chants
But the answer's still nope
And them casting don't mean to be so mean

They don't intend to offend
It just happens to happen
Again and again
And again
And again
And again
And again
Often

Yes
These eyes were once the headline eyes that read "Asian Invasion"
Yes
These eyes were once the headline eyes that read "Yellow Peril"
But today these eyes are mine
These eyes are Canadian eyes through which dreamers who went before us planted a few trees, envisioning a forest full of a lean-eyed chorus seizing each day to see the day when lean eyes are realized as real eyes
So when little lean eyes see big lean eyes on the Canadian stage
The American page
On the nine-by-sixteen letterbox widescreen
They won't be surprised but will say,

"Hey, I see those lean eyes. They kinda look like my lean eyes. Maybe one day the world will open their eyes and see me."

KOREAN ENGLISH HAIKUS *(POEMS)*

Growing up speaking both Korean and English, words played with each other between the languages. These are haikus that play at that intersection.

눈

Noon Snow Eyes Sister
At midday snowflakes cling to
My sister's eyelash

세배

Say beh Okay "Beh"
New pear Bird belly Three boats
Bowing on New Year's

차

Car Tea cha-cha-cha
Someone just cut you off Cha!
Tea Car cha-cha-cha

코

Ko Nose Board game Go
Make like a Young Jong and Ko
My cousin's nose goes

피

Pee Blood Pee Urine
Enlarged prostate? Kidney stones?
So then it's orange?

몸

Mom Body Soft Warm
She was big and now she's small
My mom's body aches

GOD IS CALLING *(POEM)*

God is calling
God is calling you
God is calling for you
God is falling for you
It's appalling how much God is stalling for you
God is calling you here to hear
To those who have ears to hear let them hear beyond me
God is calling you to hear beyond what you can see
To hear beyond seeing
Beyond receiving
Beyond reliving memories of just believing relieved to just be living rather than justly living
God is calling
So
Go
Oh
Uh oh oh no
Gotta let go to go
Those things you hold holding you, moulding you
Making you
Worry, hurry

Making you inventory
We're all born into this world grasping
Clasping tightly fisted
Knuckles twisted
Clutching clenching clinching
Inching for a taste in this insatiable race
Chasing security
Racing so fast we've erased our capacity to hear clearly
We've been raised in captivity
Praised our captivity
Embraced our captivity
Consumed by what we consume
Screens screaming and yet we're still streaming
Selling visions without meaning
Means with no end in sight
Televisions flickering light
Telling visions of sickening sights
Images projected of people protected
A mirage barrage
Appetizing to ears and eyes
Capitalizing on fears and lies
Ears in bondage
Eyes taken hostage
In the skull
Enforced to view all
Endorsed to hear all the commercials
Grabbin' and grabbin' and grabbin' and grabbin' til what
we're grabbin' is grabbin'
And it don't let go
It won't let go

We push we pull
We constantly feed but we're never full
We were tending to the garden
When our heart began to harden
When our eyes eyed that paradise prize
The wise disguise
Candidly
Underhandedly
Disbanding the fruit
Landing it at the root of our devouring mouth
Sprouting a doubt abounding out
Our eyes opened
Our eyes opened to see
To see our limit
Our smallness
Our end
No
We got so scared we thought this might be permanent
No
We got so scared we thought we'd be irrelevant
No
We got so scared we thought of things to invent, things to hold to prevent us from falling and now it's so hard to let go when God is calling
No
Where are you?
Where are you?
Where are you?

A BABY IN A MANGER *(POEM)*

A baby in a manger
Maybe a bit stranger
Maybe a baby in a manger in danger
Stranger still
For this baby in a manger in danger was, will be, is
dangerous cuz he changes us
Rearranges us
From the comic microscopic to the cosmic telescopic
Chronically kaleidoscopic
Chronologically myopic
Canonically coptic
What the heck was my topic?
(singing) Away in a manger no crib for a bed
The little lord Jesus lay down his sweet head
In a manger
Lay down his sweet head
In a mangey manger
Lay down his sweet head
In a feeding trough
Not soft
Often rough and tough wafting with smells of nasty stuff

Lay down his sweet head
In a wooden box
Framed in stocks
Built for ass and ox to feed off
To eat enough stuff
(speaking) To eat
Manger *(French)*
Manger
Manger *(French)*
Je mange
Tu manges
Il mange
Elle mange
Nous mangeons
Vous mangez
Ils mangent
Elles mangent
Jesu mange
Jesu étais mangé
Jesus eats
Jesus was eaten
Jesus was given to be eaten
Taken to be forsaken
Awaken to be spoken
Shaken to be broken to be the sacrificial token to free the captive
To enliven the imaginative
To define the divine definitive
To be that festive contemplative reminder
That active redemptive rewinder

To give sight to the blinders
Voice to the dumb
Life to the dead
Conviction to the numb
And rest to those waiting for him to come
Waiting for all this to be done
Waiting for freedom
Waiting for the ransom
Waiting for that trumpeting drum that
(singing) Pa ra pa pum pum pum
For his will to be done
For his kingdom
Come, they told me
The immaterial to the material
The impossible
The continual
The Immanuel
(speaking) Come
For unto us a child was born on Christmas morn
Descended from his throne, from his home
From the safe unknown into danger
From God, the stranger,
God became known as a baby in a manger

BARABBAS *(POEM)*

This was written during Lent in the middle of the pandemic in response to my church soliciting content. We weren't gathering in person, so, it was a way of including participation from church members. I was assigned the scene where Barabbas and Jesus are before Pontius Pilate, and thought about how Barabbas must've felt after Jesus died.

I didn't ask him to die for me
Or in my place or whatever
Y'know, it was him or me and the people made their choice
So that's not on me if you wanna get nitty gritty about it
I mean, don't get me wrong
I was grateful
Absolutely
You have no idea
Happiest day of my life
You expect to die and then you live?
Come on
Cuz it's quite the thing
Y'know, dying in public like that? Like it's a performance. And getting ready for it? Mentally? Cuz people watch you—you

at your instinctual limit—you at your extreme desperation—you at your most intense manic panic vulnerable exposure experiencing the white electric heat of the end of your life. That's what they've come to watch. Humiliation. Shame. Up there hanging for the whole world to see. I've seen it. Can't hide suffering when you're being crucified. And the prouder you are, the worse it is. The more you try to grin and bear it, the more obvious how weak you are—how weak we all are. Like, I don't know about you but I don't even like admitting I'm tired, y'know? I hide my yawns. Someone catches me nodding off, I deny it completely. It's like a form of weakness for me to admit to being tired, or hungry—I stub my toe, always pretend I'm okay. Stiff upper lip, shoulders back, chest out, keep your wits about you, show no sign of weakness cuz the wolves take out the weak ones first. Kill or be killed. Scam or be scammed. Always hack the system—never pay full price—waiting in line is for losers and everyone is a phoney so … So then imagine that, me, with that mindset, up there naked like a newborn, stuck to a cross, squirming, struggling to breathe with all those, those eyes watching. And if my enemies showed up, those whom I offended, just to make sure I was dead, yeah that's no fun—but worse than that, if my friends showed up, those who believed me? Yeah, that would hurt a lot more … but if my mom showed up, y'know? *(chuckle)* "Look, Mom, look where I ended up?" Or my dad, for that matter? I mean, my dad is a ferocious beast of a man. I didn't fall far from that tree. What would prevent him from saving me?

But then it was gone
Poof

Just like that
Jesus and I were both offered up and the people chose me
And now I'm living in the shadow of a man who died in my place

JESUS I THANK YOU *(SONG)*

This was written in a Makers Collective in response to Psalm 9.

Jesus
I thank you
For these faces that I see
When we're Zooming with each other
I feel you smiling down on me

Jesus
I thank you
For this most amazing day
We were looking through screens dimly
But now we're seeing face to face
Face to face

Jesus
You broke through
And shined your light on me
I felt trapped alone in a darkness
And you slowly set me free

Jesus
You held me
And carried me through this year
By the hands of my new friends
You answered my prayer
You answered my prayer

Turns out you were listening
You were always there
You were desperately seeking me
Turns out you heard all my cries
As I frantically tried
To stop you from holding me
Turns out in the crux
Of my panic and pain
When I, in distress
Couldn't cope or maintain
You were right there
In the wind and the rain
With me in the storm
Calling my name

Jesus
Please keep me
So I might stay right here
And never leave this place
This awareness
That you are always near

Jesus
You're my best friend
Descended from above
May I be a friend to others
As a vessel of your love
May I be a friend to others
As a vessel of your love

ALWAYS WRITING

I never used to like writing. Writing came with a bunch of rules I didn't understand. I never knew how to start, how to end, what to do in the middle, spelling, grammar—writing was a panic-inducing activity trying to hide behind a pile of stolen words. Whenever I wrote, I wasn't pursuing something, I was just trying not to make a mistake.

I didn't like writing cuz I didn't think I was any good at it. No one ever complimented my writing. Which is fair. I probably never wrote anything worth complimenting. But when I was a kid, I won a singing contest once. It was a Toronto Korean church thing, so, not that many contestants, but still, I received the first-place trophy and it felt great—people applauded, took pictures, complimented me and smiled. My mom bought me a Quarter Pounder with Cheese at McDonald's as a reward. I never got a Quarter Pounder with Cheese. That was for rich folks. But there I was, mowing down on this rich people food cuz I sang a song. I still love singing. All that to say, if someone bought me a Quarter Pounder with Cheese after I wrote something when I was kid I probably would've gotten into writing sooner.

Another reason why I didn't like writing when I was a kid was cuz I didn't like reading. I don't think I read a book til like, grade seven? I remember reading *The Outsiders* by S. E. Hinton in grade seven—okay, fine, I remember seeing the movie after being assigned the book to read for class. I think I didn't read much cuz I couldn't read fast. I'm still a slow reader and I'm fine with that now, but for some reason, when I was a kid, speed meant you were better—faster runners won, the first one to finish their plate got seconds at dinner. When I tried reading fast, I'd stumble over the words and couldn't remember anything I'd just read.

In high school I remember slowly reading J. D. Salinger's *The Catcher in the Rye*, C. S. Lewis's *Mere Christianity* and Mary Shelley's *Frankenstein*. And for some reason, I connected with those writers—across time and culture, their words slowly reached me.

Regardless of how I feel, I try to write every day—at home, in a library, at a café—lately I've been writing in food courts between breakfast and lunch. I dunno, something about the public din of food courts speaks to me. I try to write non-stop for three, four hours, then go for a walk. But sometimes I don't feel like writing, so I refuse myself food until I finish a chunk. Like a reward. Or I buy a ticket to a movie for later if I do some writing now. And if I get too busy writing, I skip the movie and it was worth it. If I can finagle a deadline that involves me sharing my writing with real people, that's the best. But without deadlines, it's difficult to feel the progress—I need to push up against something.

My first draft of anything is terrible. But that's okay. Cuz the purpose of the first draft is not to be good, it's to provide your future self with something to edit. That's the goal. So do your future self a favour and fill the page right now.

Writing has become a process of discovery for me rather than expression. It's not as if I have something in my head to write and then I write it. It's in the act of writing itself where I discover—where I reveal to myself, as I write—what it is I wanna say.

We're all encouraged to write creatively when we're kids and then we slowly fill up our schedules and suddenly can't afford to spare the time. Sure, some people have natural inclinations toward one thing or another and a handful are touched by God in a unique way, but for most of us, it's usually a matter of simply being invited to write and given a deadline.

You don't ever hear about building confidence through writing. Or building character, faith, an identity, patience, empathy, community … but that's what writing has done for me.

Writing, thank you.

P.S. And now you're all cordially invited to write something creative, and in two weeks you gotta share it with someone who loves you.

JOY *(SONG)*

This was written during Advent in the middle of the pandemic in response to my church soliciting content. I was assigned the word Joy.

I tried writing a serious song
Then this song came along
Hope you enjoy this Choiful song
About everything that rhymes with Joy.

    Baby Jesus was a boy
    I'm allergic to soy
    My uncle's name is Roy
    This is my favourite toy

    Helen of Troy
    Some say she was an envoy
    Who might've been employed as a decoy to help destroy
    the city of Troy

I tried writing a serious song
Then this song came along

Hope you enjoy this Choiful song
About everything that rhymes with Joy.

Some British people say "Oi"
To a Jew I'm a goy
Pirates say "Ahoy."
The French say "Moy" (I think it's pronounced "moi")

Did you see the movie *Tommy Boy*
Chris Farley was the real McCoy
I think he loved wearing corduroy
Like a cowboy
Eating bokchoy in Illinois

I never saw the Bolshoi
But I think I did see *The Drawer Boy*
I read a book written by Tolstoy
I think it was called *Rob Roy*
No it wasn't called *Rob Roy*
But I saw a movie 'bout the Beach Boys
And a documentary about Christian Hosoi
This microphone contains nickel alloy

Baby Jesus was a boy
I'm allergic to soy
My uncle's name is Roy
This is my favourite toy
I enjoy to annoy my sister with a ploy

I tried writing a serious song
Then this song came along
Hope you enjoy this Choiful song
About everything that rhymes with Joy.

© Ryan Jinn

INS CHOI is an actor, poet and playwright. His first play, *Kim's Convenience*, won Best New Play and the Patrons' Pick Award at the 2011 Toronto Fringe Festival. Since then, it has been produced multiple times in Canada, the UK and the US to sold-out runs and rave reviews. It was adapted into a TV series of the same name on CBC and Netflix for five seasons, where Choi was a writer, executive producer and co-creator. He has also written the plays *Subway Stations of the Cross* and *Bad Parent* and collectively created *2000 Candles* (Brookstone), *Window on Toronto*, *Alligator Pie* and *(re)Birth: e. e. cummings in Song* (Soulpepper). Born in South Korea, Choi grew up in Scarborough, and now resides in Toronto with his wife and their two screenagers.